Books By Jessica Kristie

Winter Dress

Letters of Capitulation

Threads of Life

Dreaming in Darkness

Barbed-Wire Butterflies (fiction)

Winter Goose Publishing
45 Lafayette Road #114
North Hampton, NH 03862

wintergoosepublishing.com
Contact Information: info@wintergoosepublishing.com

Unwritten Things

COPYRIGHT © 2025 by Jessica Kristie

Cover Design and Formatting by Winter Goose Publishing

ISBN: 978-1-952909-33-7

Published in the United States of America

To My Rib . . .

the soul connection that tugs at me in this moment and the next.
May we live differently in the next lifetime—but love just as deeply.
We are the same, and I miss you in every timeline.

Contents

My Hunger

Forbidden

Holy

The Reckoning

Almost Yours

My Hunger

If You Were Mine

If you were mine—
I'd memorize the map of your breath,
where it catches when you crave me
but won't say it.
I'd trace the soft defiance
in your lips,
until they forgot how to lie
about not needing this.

You look at me
like the night looks at the moon—
longing,
but never daring to reach.
And I wear that look
like silk on bare skin,
letting it slide into places
you've only dreamed of entering.

We speak in what-ifs,
in half-sentences
and glances that burn down the hours.
But silence is a terrible liar—
and mine is always calling your name.

So I'll keep you
as the pulse beneath my ribs,
a beautiful wound

that never heals,
cherishing the pain
as proof
that once,
I felt something
too profound to hold.

If You Asked

If you asked,
I would give you everything.
Every line I've ever written
in the dark,
every pain I've carried
like armor.

I would bleed on your page
if it meant you'd understand
how deeply I feel you.

You are the place
I rest my unrest.
The space between my chaos.
The only silence
that doesn't ask me to explain.

I want to come undone in your hands.
Not for pleasure,
but for truth.
So you can know me
in the places I've never shown
anyone else.
The places even I
have tried to bury.

You make me want
to hand it all over—

the bruises,
the softness,
the burning need
to be known
without being fixed.

And maybe it's reckless,
but I'd rather be ruined by you
than preserved by someone
who never looked deeper
than my smile.

So, if you asked—
God,
if you asked…

I would give you
everything.

Quiet Hours

It's always the quiet hours
that hurt the most—
when the world softens,
and I realize
how long it's been
since I was held
without hesitation.

I ache for something
I'm not sure I believe in anymore—
gentle hands,
uncomplicated warmth,
a voice that stays
without needing a reason.

But the past still lives in me,
a ghost with perfect timing,
whispering
don't trust this,
don't hope for too much,
you remember how this ends.

And I do.
All of me does.

But still—
some part of me lights a candle
every night.

Just in case
someone sees the flicker
and comes in
from the dark.

Too Much Like Truth

I'm loud,
honest
in all the ways I can be.

But you scare me.

I love like wildfire—
no hesitation,
no second guessing,
just open palms
and a heart
that doesn't know
how to hold back.

And I've never touched anything
that didn't question
or fade
or ask me to be less.

But you—
you make me feel whole
and *more*.
And that kind of power
terrifies me.

I've wanted you
in every way.
Dreamed of the way you'd fall apart

under my hands,
how your body would sound
wrapped around my name.

But this—
you—
you're too much like truth.
And I don't know
what to do with something
that doesn't ask to be earned,
but simply given.

So I keep my distance.
Not because I don't want you—
but because I do.
So deeply,
it cracks something in me.

And I don't want to ruin
the only thing
that's ever seen me clearly
and stayed.

I'll Wait Here

I don't want someone else.
Not their hands,
not their voice,
not their hollow promise
of maybe.

I want you.

The way your rhythm changes
when you're close.
The way your silence feels
like a tether
wrapped around my ribs.

I want the life we imagine
when no one's looking.
The nights you trace my name
on skin
you're not supposed to touch.

I'd rather hurt for you
than lie beside someone
who doesn't make me burn.

I'd rather wait—
half-wild,
half-wrecked,
drenched in longing—

than let someone else
fill the space
you still live in.

Because this isn't a crush.
It's not infatuation.
It's not hope.

It's knowing.
In my body.
In my blood.
In the place between thought and burning,
where you already live.

So take your time.

I'll wait here—
brimming with want,
wrapped in your memory,
unmoved by anyone
who isn't you.

Never Had To Ask

I would give you my rib
if it meant you'd breathe easier.
Let you live beneath each layer
if it meant I could keep you safe.

I'd change cities.
Change names.
Burn the map
and follow only the scent of you.

I'd learn your streets,
your rhythms,
the way your shoulder tastes
at midnight
and how your chest rises
when you sleep.

You don't know
how much I ache
just to be close enough
to feel your warmth
without asking.

I'd strip my life bare
just to build one beside you—
one with no guessing,
no distance,

no quiet rooms
without your scent in them.

I would bend,
not because I'm weak,
but because love like this
demands movement.
Demands offering.
And if you asked—
for a piece of me,
for all of me,
for just one life
where I could reach you
whenever I needed to—
I'd say yes
before the words
even left
your lips.

No One Else

They ask why I'm alone.
Why I don't move on.
Why I let months pass
with no new memories
pressing to my chest.

And I smile—
because they don't know
what it's like
to be ruined
by the right person.

You touched me
like I was meant for it.
Not just my movements—
but all the quiet,
wild
aching
parts of me
I don't show to anyone else.

Now I live
half here,
half in fantasy,
still trembling
from a name I can't say out loud.

I don't want to be touched
by anyone
who doesn't look at me
like you do—
like I am gravity,
like I am fire,
like I am yours.

So no,
I'm not waiting for love.
I have it.
I'm just not willing
to pretend
that anyone else
fits.

Before Your Hands

I loved you
before your hands found my thighs.
Before your voice
curled around my frame
like a secret.

Before your mouth
pressed to mine,
and time unraveled
in the heat between us.

I loved you
before you were inside me.
Before the ache became sacred.
Before I knew
what it would feel like
to come apart
in your arms
and never want to be whole again.

It wasn't the way you twisted around me.
It was the way you saw me—
the unspoken knowing,
the gravity,
the pull.

You could've never touched me at all
and still—
I would've belonged to you.

My body was just the last place
you arrived.
My heart,
my breath,
my every quiet
yes—

You had all of it
long before
you ever asked.

Forbidden

Unspoken Desires

In the quiet corners of my mind,
I find you—a forbidden thought,
A whisper of what could be,
Entwined with the echoes of restraint.

Your presence lingers like a shadow,
A constant reminder of boundaries drawn,
Yet the heart yearns for what it cannot have,
A dance on the edge of propriety.

We exchange glances, fleeting and charged,
Words left unsaid, heavy with meaning,
A delicate balance of desire and decorum,
Navigating the labyrinth of our emotions.

But some paths are best left unexplored,
Some fires left unlit,
For the cost of indulgence may be too great,
And the weight of consequence, too heavy to bear.

Unattainable

In the hush of midnight's embrace,
I conjure the warmth of your unseen reach,
A forbidden current coursing through my veins,
Igniting desires I dare not voice aloud.

Your presence lingers in the shadows,
A tantalizing whisper against my flesh,
A reminder of boundaries we cannot cross,
Yet in dreams, I taste the sweetness of your lips.

We navigate this delicate dance,
A symphony of stolen looks and unspoken words,
Our hearts entwined in a clandestine waltz,
Yearning for a union that remains just out of reach.

But reality's chains bind us tight,
And though my soul whispers for your embrace,
I cherish the torment of this impossible love,
For even in longing, I find a bittersweet solace.

Between the Lines

In the hush of stolen moments,
we find solace in the language of touch,
where words falter and boundaries blur.
Your fingertips, familiar yet forbidden,
trace constellations upon my chest,
mapping desires we've left unspoken.

We exist in fragments—
a collection of midnight encounters
and whispered confessions
that dissolve with the dawn.
Each embrace a paradox,
satisfying yet kindling a deeper hunger,
a yearning for more than the night allows.

Your lips press promises
they cannot keep,
leaving imprints of longing
that linger long after you've gone.
And I, caught in this endless loop
of passion and restraint,
wonder if the echoes of our union
haunt you as they do me.

If Not This Life

If not this life—
then the next.
Because what we have
isn't something you feel
and forget.

You see through me
like you've lived in this skin before.
Like you built it.
Like your lips
were made to name
what no one else could reach.

We fit
in all the ways that matter,
except time.

You taste like fate—
but I have to keep swallowing you
like a secret.

And God,
I would ruin every plan I made
just to lie beside you
without guilt.

But we met
mid-story.

Mid-burn.
Mid-promise
to someone else
or some other path
that we swore we'd stay loyal to.

And I know
if we let this go,
it won't leave us.
It'll haunt the quiet moments.
The almosts.
The what-ifs.
The next time someone says our name
with less meaning.

We are the same fire
with different homes.
And maybe this lifetime
isn't built for the blaze
we'd become.

But I love you.
Because you see me.
Because I see you.
Because some connections
don't care
about permission.

What We're Not

You come to me
wrapped in heat and hesitation,
a body that knows mine
better than it should.
We speak in sighs, in fingertips,
in the quiet throb of everything
we can't be in daylight.

I taste you in the pauses—
between your words,
between your loyalty
and what you lose
when you undress for me.

This isn't love,
not the kind we can speak,
but I feel it in your breath
when it stumbles
at the edge of goodbye.
You stay long enough
to remind me what I'm not,
then leave before it feels like more.

And still, I crave you—
not the touch
(though it's everything),
but the version of you
I'll never get to keep.

If You Loved Me

If you loved me—
you'd leave.
You'd burn it down.
You'd show up
with nothing but your name
and say,
This is what I choose.

But you never do.
You fuck me
like it's a secret blessing,
like I should thank you
for breaking me
gently.

You say,
You know this isn't simple,
and I say,
It never needed to be.

I only ever bent
for you.
Just you.
But I guess that was the most
complicated thing of all.

Even When You're Not Here

You're not here.
But somehow,
you are.

In the way I exhale
like you're listening.
In the way my body still reacts
to your name,
your rhythm,
your silence.

I feel you
in the calm that finds me
after everyone else has left.
When I finally stop pretending
I'm fine without you.

You live
in the songs on repeat.
In the lines I don't speak aloud
because they sound too much
like us.

There are hours
where I forget you're not mine.
Where the world feels warmer
just from thinking
of the way you see me—

without filters,
without asking me to be less.

And even though your hands
aren't on me,
I still feel held.

Even when your voice
is just a memory,
I still hear the way
you made me feel real.

You're not here.
But love like this
doesn't disappear.
It just lives differently.
In whispers.
In blood.
In everything I am
when I think of you.

What I Don't Say

I love you.
More than I should.
More than makes sense
for what we are—
for what we're allowed to be.

But it's not something I chose.
It just happened.
In your voice.
In the way you see me.
In the space between your words
where I feel safe
for no reason
and every reason.

I know I'll never have you
in the way I want.
Not completely.
Not without consequence.

And still,
I'd take every half-moment,
every hidden exchange,
every late-night echo of you
just to feel close
to something that's real.

You say I mean more to you
than you can explain.
That if things were different…

But they're not.
And I live in that.
Every day.

I never ask for more.
But the stars know,

I ache for it.

Because this love—
this unspoken, undone,
undeniable thing between us—
is the most beautiful hurt
I've ever known.

What We Keep

We don't talk about it,
not really.
But it's in every message.
Every glance.
Every pause
where the truth almost spills
but doesn't.

You call me
when the noise quiets.
When the rest of your life
has stopped demanding
so much of you.
And I answer—
I'll always answer.

We hold each other
in the in-between.
In the texts sent
but never said aloud.
In the softness
we save
just for each other.

You have another life.
A whole world
you promised before me.

And I don't ask you
to choose.
I just let you come back
in the ways that you can.

Because what we have
isn't something
that fits into lines.
Or titles.
Or timing.

It's something we keep
quietly.
Sacred.
Burning
just beneath
the scar

of every ordinary day.

Only When it Rains

You show up
when the sky splits open,
storm in your eyes,
your ring catching light
like a threat.

We don't talk,
we undress.
Conversation would make it real,
and we've both agreed—
this isn't real.
It's just need.
It's just night.
It's just us.

Your reach doesn't ask permission—
it remembers.
And I open,
not like a flower,
but like a wound
that's missed the blade.

You take me like I'm yours.
Like I've always been.
But when morning peeks in,
your voice returns
to something measured,

your kiss
to something colder.

I don't cry anymore.
Not when you leave,
not when you lie,
not when you pretend
I was never there.

But the rain always knows.
It taps on my window
like your fingers once did,
reminding me—
you only come
when the sky remembers
how to fall.

What We Don't Say

You look at me
like I'm a decision
you already made,
and regret
in equal measure.

We never speak about it—
souls connected.
But it hangs between us
like smoke,
like the kind of truth
that scorches everything it reaches.

You say my name
like it's sacred,
then go home
to a life you promised
before you ever knew
what I would do to you.

I let you hold me
like you're drowning.

And I'll stay here—
soaked in the echo,
smelling of you,
saying nothing

because saying everything
would ruin what little
we get to keep.

Not Mine

You tell me
you don't love me—
but your gasps say otherwise.
So does the way
you stay too long,
and the silence you sit in
when I ask nothing at all.

We don't have a song,
a photo,
a future.
But we have this:
the kind of heat
that makes the world go still,
makes guilt feel
like a distant echo.

You love me
in the way you can—
in gasps, in glances,
in the pause before
you put your ring back on.

And I take it,
every fractured second,

because I don't know
how not to want
what was never mine.

After

You never say goodbye.
Just disappear.
Like I was a fever
you finally broke.

I don't call.
I don't text.
I let the silence
be what it is—
a mirror,
a grave,
a goddamn relief.

But some nights,
when I've convinced myself
you were nothing more
than a lesson,
I remember the way
you whispered my name
into the hollow of my neck—
like it meant something.
Like I did.

And I hate that part of me
still believes
you meant it.

Room 915

We never say where we're going,
but the room knows us.
It smells like our secrets now.
Like sweat and apology.

You take your time
like it's a favor,
undressing me
like I'm both privilege and punishment.

We don't talk about her,
but she's there—
in the pauses,
in the way you never look me in the eye
when I ask if you're staying.

You say,
"I don't know how to stop this."
I smile like I'm not breaking.
I pull you back into me
and let the silence
have its way.

The Lie We Live In

You love me.
I know.
I feel it in the way you fall apart
every time I tell you to leave.

But you won't say it.
Not out loud.
Because saying it
would make it real,
and real is where things
get ruined.

So we stay in the in-between—
half-truths and whole bodies,
soft moans under harsh lights,
you kissing me
like redemption,
then zipping up guilt
and going home.

And me—
still here,
still craving
the version of you
you only become
when we're pretending
this is nothing.

The Space Between

You never say you love me.
But you kiss like a man who does,
and fuck like a man who can't.

There's a moment—
right after,
when your head rests against my chest,
when your breath slows,
when your silence is louder
than anything you've ever said.

And I pretend it's enough.
That this skin
isn't starving for soul.
That your chest
doesn't tremble
with everything you've buried.

We lie there,
in the space between
what we desire
and what we're allowed.
And I wonder
if I'll ever be more
than your favorite mistake.

Tethered

You say this isn't love—
not the kind that lasts,
not the kind that makes it
to the light of day.

But you stay longer now.
You linger.
You text after.
You ask what I'm doing
when you know damn well
you can't be part of it.

I think you need to be mine.
But you already belong to someone else,
and I've stopped trying
to make sense of a heart
that beats for two homes.

Still, you leave something behind every time—
a shirt,
a silent whimper,
a look that says,
don't love me,
but also,
don't stop.

This Is How It Ends

Not with a fight.
Not with a confession.
But with another slow undoing.

Your embrace still fits mine
like it was made for it,
but your eyes are already
somewhere else.

You say,
"I can't do this anymore."
And I nod
like I wasn't still waiting
for you to finally choose me.

You kiss me
like a man trying to forget
what goodbye tastes like.

And when you leave,
you don't look back.
But I do.
Because someone has to remember
the way it felt
to be loved
in secret.

The Things You Don't Say

You tell me how much you long for me
like it's supposed to be enough.
Like my thighs
can replace promises,
like my mouth
can silence the scream
of never being chosen.

You don't say love.
But you say need.
You say I can't stay long.
You say this has to end.
But then your hands
learn me all over again,
and your eyes
says everything your mouth never will.

And me—
I let it happen.
I swallow the silence
like it might become something
if I just hold it long enough.

The Smell of Him

He always smells like cologne
and a place I'll never belong.
Like warm skin
and a life
that ends at someone else's dinner table.

I wear him for hours
after he's gone—
his sweat,
his sighs,
his indecision.

I should wash him off.
But I like the way it hurts
to still feel him.

I like the lie
that lingers on my neck
long after
his truth walks out the door.

Where We Go

You touch me
like I'm more memory than skin,
like your palms know
what your mouth still won't admit.

We don't speak much in the dark—
just breath,
just friction,
just the sound of intention
disguised as control.

I get lost in it.
The heat.
The hush.
The way pain turns to pleasure
when it's wrapped in your voice.

We go somewhere else here—
somewhere time doesn't find us,
where guilt doesn't knock,
and the only truth
is how deep we can fall
without saying a word.

The Way You Look at Me

You look at me
like I'm the answer
to something you didn't know
you were asking.

Your eyes
burn more than your touch,
and when you're inside me,
you're softer
than you let anyone see.

I feel the war in you—
the pull between
I want this
and
I shouldn't.
And I let you fight it
while I give in.

Because in that moment,
you're mine.
No titles.
No past.
Just breath.
And heat.

And the promise
that maybe love doesn't always
have to come with light.

Bruised Beautiful

There's something bruised
about the way we move—
like we're both aching
for something
we've never quite found
in anyone else.

I don't know if this is love,
but I know it's something.
Something that leaves marks
on more than just our flesh.

Your fingers dig in
like you're trying to stay grounded,
and I let you,
even when it hurts,
because sometimes
pain is the only thing
that makes us feel real.

We were never meant
to be gentle.
But we do know

how to burn.

Take

You don't ask—
you take,
but not in a way that hurts.
You take like a man
who's been starving for years
and just found water.

There's reverence in it,
even when it's rough.
Like you're worshipping
what you can't keep.

And I let you.
Every time.
Because I know
you'll leave before morning,
but here,
in this drenched silence,
I matter.

Not as a woman you love.
But as one
you can't forget.

Your Mouth on My Name

You say my name
like it's not yours to have—
slow,
ragged,
like confession.

And in the dark,
when your voice
is the only thing I hear,
it sounds almost like love.

Almost.

Your lips move
from my name
to my skin,
and I can't tell
if you're trying to drown me
or save yourself.

Either way,
I opened like a wound
and called it mercy.

The Way We Break

It's not precious,
not careful—
this thing between us.

It's hands
digging into hips.
It's mouths
that know too much.
It's moans
that sound like mourning.

We don't make love.
We unravel.
And somewhere in the tangle,
I forget
why I should be afraid.

You hold me
like something sacred
and ruined.

And for a moment,
we both believe
this could be more
than just a beautiful way
to break.

Ruin Me Right

You don't say
you want me—
you just reach.
And I let you.
Every damn time.

There's something holy
about the way you undo me—
hands reverent,
mouth blasphemous.

You know exactly
how to break me open.
Not with violence,
but with precision—
the kind of ruin
that feels like grace.

And I don't ask for promises.
Just this.
This moment.
This burn.
This knowing
that for a little while,
you forget everything
but me.

Only Here

You're only mine
in this room,
in this bed,
in this movement less dark
where nothing outside exists.

Here,
you touch me
like I'm truth.
Like I'm the answer
you weren't supposed to need.

You press against me louder
than anything your lips
will ever admit.

And I've stopped needing the words.
Because I know—
in the way your hips meet mine,
in the way your arms tremble
when I say your name—
that whatever this is,
it's real.
Even if it's only real
in the places
no one else can see.

In the Tangle

We don't talk about
what this means.
We just find each other—
again,
again,
again.

Your warmth lingers on my neck,
your fingers in my hair,
your weight—
a gravity I can't fight.

I don't want gentle.
I want consumed.
I want to be the place you go
when everything else
feels too quiet.

And you—
you want to be lost.
To disappear
inside the heat,
the noise,
the skin of someone
who doesn't ask
for anything
but now.

So we tangle.
And we ache.
And we pretend
this isn't more
than it is.

But we both know,
that it is.

What We Left in The Flames

We don't speak enough.
But I know you feel me.
That hush in your chest
when certain songs play.
That flicker
when a scent drags my name
out of nowhere.

I feel it too.
In the pauses between days.
In the way no one else
has touched the places
you cracked open
just by seeing me.

We weren't made to last.
But we were made.
You can't unwrite a collision.
You can't unlove
what carved itself
into your blood.

We tore through each other
like we didn't believe in limits.
Loved like the world might end
before morning.

And in some ways,
it did.

But even now—
long after the fire,
long after the smoke—
I still find pieces of us
in the ash.

And no,
I wouldn't go back.
Not to the crash,
not to the chaos.

But I also wouldn't forget.
Because something about us
was truer
than anything I've ever had since.

We left each other
in the flames.
But part of me
still glows
because of you.

I Know What This Is

I don't need to be reminded
that you're not mine.
That the life you return to
isn't the one we imagined
in stolen breaths
and almosts.

I know what this is.
I know what it isn't.

And still,
I love you.
With a gentleness
that aches.
With a reverence
that doesn't ask
to be seen.

You don't need to say it.
Not out loud.
I feel it
in the way you hesitate
before hanging up.
In the quiet
that lingers after goodbye
like it doesn't want to leave either.

We were never going to be forever.
We were just going to be real.

And that's what hurts the most—
that love
can be this deep,
this true,
and still not be something
we get to keep.

But I'll carry it.
Not like a weight,
but like a warmth
I return to
when the world feels cold.

Because even if this love
wasn't meant to last—
it was meant.
And that,
I'll never erase.

Beautiful Wreckage

We were never soft.
We met like impact—
steel on steel,
heat against heat,
two restless souls
meant to collide exactly like this.

You're not safe.
Neither am I.
But somehow,
we made each other feel
like home
in the middle of the fire.

We are chaos—
but the kind that leaves
everything more honest
in its wake.
We strip each other
down to bone,
to truth,
to the trembling parts
we hide from the rest of the world.

If you're a train wreck,
then I'm the smoke

still rising
from everything we burned.

And yet—
what a ride.
What a fucking beautiful
collision.

Because without you,
my tracks would be quiet.
My cars would run cold.
My journey
wouldn't hum with the ache
of something so deeply
meant.

Ours is the kind of love
that teaches,
even as it scars.
That destroys,
but still rebuilds.

I don't need soft.
I need real.
And you—
you are the most devastating
truth
I've ever loved.

You, Every Time

I was never looking for peace.
Not really.
Not the kind that comes from silence,
from standing still,
from being good.

I was built for motion.
For mess.
For more.

And then there was you.
All fire and sharp corners.
All the kind of truth
that peeled me open without permission.

You didn't fix me.
You didn't try.
You saw the smoke,
the twisted rails,
and ran straight into the wreck anyway.

God, you're chaos.
But you're *my* chaos.
The only kind that ever felt
like breath.

Without you,
my tracks mean nothing.

Just lines drawn
toward nowhere.
You gave my direction purpose.
Even if we both knew
we were speeding
toward the edge.

I don't regret a second of it.
Not the crashes.
Not the damage.
Not the scars.

Because you're the one thing
I'd break for again.
And again.
And again.

Not every love
was meant to survive.

But this one?
It was meant to happen.

And if I had the chance—
I'd still crash into you.
Every time.

Everywhere You Aren't

I feel you
in the songs I skip
because they say too much.

In the quiet
right before sleep
when my heart is loud
with things I'll never tell you.

You're everywhere
you're not supposed to be—
in my thoughts,
in my dreams,
in the parts of me
I promised to keep safe
from wanting.

I don't want a piece of you.
I want all of it—
the late-night thoughts,
the half-healed scars,
the way your voice breaks
when you're trying to be strong.

But I know better
than to ask the world
for something it's not ready to give.

So I carry you
quietly.
Permanently.
Like a scar I wouldn't trade,
even if it still stings
when I press on it.

Because some people
aren't lost—
they're just not yours
to hold in this lifetime.

Holy

You Never Knew

You kissed me
like it was the beginning.
But I was already
yours.

You thought it was just residue.
Just heat.
Just another moment
to claim.

But I had already
poured myself into you.
In the way I whispered.
In the way I softened.
In the way I stilled
when your breath
met my neck
like a promise.

You grabbed me
with hands that didn't know
they were holding
everything.

And I still let you.
Because loving you
felt holy,

even if you never realized
you were on sacred ground.

You'll look back someday
and remember the way
I flowed
without asking anything in return.
The way my eyes
told you
what my mouth never begged for.

You'll remember.
And it'll hurt.

Because I loved you
completely—
before you ever understood
what you had.

Built From My Rib

You fit
like something carved
from the inside of me—
not held,
but *remembered*.

I feel you
in the parts of me
that were never touched
until you walked in.

You didn't need to ask
for my loyalty.
My body knew
before my mind did.
Before you ever said my name
like it meant something.

You were never a stranger.
Just a piece
that wandered too far
before finding its way back.

If God built you from my rib,
He buried you deep.
Somewhere beneath the soft
and the wild,

in the place I protect
with teeth.

And maybe that's why
I break like this—
not from lack,
but from recognition.
From the way your absence
feels like something missing
from me.

Not broken.
Not incomplete.
Just made for something
I can't quite reach,
but will always feel.

Because love like this
isn't learned.
It's remembered.
Bone by bone.

Because It Hurts Good

I don't come back
because I believe in you.
I come back
because the way you handle me
makes everything else disappear.

You don't ask
if I'm okay.
You ask
how deep I can take it.
And I lie—
because I want to be the kind of woman
who can take all of you
without thought.

But the truth?
It hurts.
Not just the pull,
not just the breathlessness—
but the knowing
that this is the only way
you'll ever let me feel close.
And still,
I beg for it.
Because at least
it feels
like something real.

The Hours We Steal

You arrive like thunder—
loud in my veins,
silent in the world we return to.
There's no voice for this,
what we do in borrowed time,
but my bones call it devotion.

You fuck like you're searching for something—
maybe the version of yourself
you can't find at home.
And I take you in
like penance,
like prayer,
like I might be the answer
you'll never let yourself want.

We don't speak of knots.
It would ruin the ritual—
the way your hands confess
what your mouth never will,
the way you say goodbye
like it costs you nothing.

But I know better.
I feel it in the way you pause
before walking away,
as if the echo of me

follows you
long after the door shuts.

We are beautiful
in the most broken ways,
tangled in everything we pretend
is just surface,
when it's always been
so much more.

No One Else Gets This

You say my name
like it's a secret—
low, rough,
meant for inside me,
not the air.

And when we move,
it's not slow,
it's not soft—
it's desperate.
It's messy.
It's holy.

You bury yourself in me
like you're trying
to forget her name.
And I let you—
not because I don't know
what this is,
but because I do.

No one else gets this.
Not like we do.
Not this restlessness
not this silence,
not this craving
with claws.

We were made
for this kind
of ruin.

The Ache Stays

After,
you leave like you always do—
quiet,
efficient,
unreached.

I lie there
still trembling,
still open,
still half full
of something that felt
a lot like worship.

And I tell myself
I'm okay.
That I wanted this.
That it's better this way.

But the tremble stays.
Not in my body—
it knows how to recover.
In my chest.
In the place that thought,
Maybe this time,
he won't pull away so fast.

He Prays in My Body

You never kneel in churches,
but you kneel for me.

Mouth open,
breath reverent,
like I'm something divine
you're trying to make sense of
with your tongue.

You worship me
in the dark,
when no one's watching,
when no vows can be broken
because they were never said out loud.

And I let you.
Because it feels holy
to be wanted
like this.

But holy things
aren't meant to bleed—
and I'm always
the one left open.

Holy things
aren't supposed to yearn—

and I've mistaken pain
for prayer
before.

Half of You

I only get the version
you don't show to the world—
the undone one,
the one who whispers love
like it's a curse
and fucks like its redemption.

You call it complicated.
I call it cowardice.
But still, I wait—
bare and burning,
for the scraps of softness
you tuck beneath your shame.

You kiss me like I'm holy,
then vanish like a sin.
And I keep letting you,
because I've tasted the truth
inside your lies,
and it's the sweetest goddamn thing
I've ever known.

We are bruises
masquerading as soulmates.
We are fire
no one's willing to claim.

And still—
in the silence after,
when you exhale into me
scents of regret,
I let myself believe
you might come back
different.

You won't.
But I love the part of you
that almost could.

Altar

I built you an altar
inside my chest—
fed it with silence,
kept it burning
every time you left
and came back
just to kneel
and take.

You offered no prayers.
Only need.
Only hunger.
Only a voice for me
that sounded like praise
but felt like possession.

And I mistook that
for devotion.
Mistook you
breaking into me
as proof
that I was sacred.

But I see it now.
You never came to worship.
Only to be forgiven.

Lay Me Bare

I don't want to be careful with you.
I want to be real.
Ugly, raw,
aching in all the places
I usually hide.

I want to take the polished version of me—
the one the world accepts—
and strip her down
at your feet.

Let you see the mess.
The madness.
The face that asks for too much
and the heart that never learned
how to need quietly.

I want you to know what it means
to be inside a soul like mine.
To trace the edges of my wounds
without pain.
To love me, not in spite of them—
but because of them.

I would let you read the pages
no one else gets to witness.
The ones I only write
when I'm falling apart.

And if you asked me
to give myself to you,
not just the curves,
but my undoing—
I would.

Because with you,
I don't need to be contained.
I don't need to be palatable.
I just need to be
real.

So lay me bare.
Not to fix.
Not to claim.
Just to know
what it feels like
to be fully seen
and still wanted.

If You Touched Me

If you touched me—
not just skin,
but the part of me
that shrinks
when love gets too close—
I think I'd break.
And I think I'd thank you for it.

I imagine your bones
like gravity—
pulling truth from me
I didn't know I still carried.
Undoing the knots
I tied around my softness
to survive.

If you touched me
like you meant it—
slow,
with intention,
with the knowing of someone
who's lived inside my ache—
I think I'd finally understand
what it means
to be held
instead of handled.

Not claimed.
Not owned.
But kept,
in the kind of way
that makes staying
feel like freedom.

I wonder
if you know
what your touch could do
to a woman like me—
not just what's sacred,
but to all the rooms inside me
that have been waiting
to be entered
without force.

If you touched me
like that—
I wouldn't run.

I'd unlock
and open.

Anyway

I know this won't change a thing.
I know you'll still belong
to a life that isn't mine.
To promises I wasn't there to witness
but still feel bound by.

And yet—
I offer myself
like prayer.
Like maybe love,
even unspoken,
still deserves to be known.

I don't give you this
to make you choose.
I give you this
because I don't know how
to love you
in halves.

You reach for me
with careful hands.
I fall into them
like I was born to.
Even if I know
they'll let go
before morning.

You say nothing
because there's nothing safe
left to say.

And I don't ask.
Because I already know.

This collision
won't change your world.
But it's changed mine.

So I kiss you
like it's the last time.
Because it might be.
Because it always is.

And I give you
everything I shouldn't—
again,
anyway.

The Fire We Don't Touch

You love me.
I see it in the way
your voice softens
when you say my name.
In the pauses
where your body hesitates
to walk away.

I love you too—
so much
it aches beneath my ribs.
So much
I'd burn this whole world
if it meant keeping you
for one unruined day.

But we both know
this fire isn't safe.
It's sacred,
but it's not ours to hold.
Not in this life.
Not like we want.

So we touch
like thieves.
Mouths heavy
with everything we can't say.

Fingers tracing lines
we never get to follow.

You take your time with me
like you're memorizing
a dream
you'll have to wake from.
And I let you.
I let you have all of me
in the dark—
because daylight
doesn't belong to us.

And when it's over,
we don't cry.
We don't speak.
We just lay there,
skin to skin,
hearts breaking
in perfect unison.

This love is real.
But it isn't free.

And no matter how deep
we bury ourselves in each other—
we still come up
starving.

Still Inside Me

You're gone—
but not really.
I still feel you
in the places
I opened
just for you.

My skin remembers.
The weight of your hands.
The way your breath caught
when I let you in
without flinching.

We didn't say love.
We didn't have to.
It was there
in every pause
we didn't fill with words.
In every touch
that asked for nothing
but everything.

You moved in me
like you belonged there.
And maybe you did.
Maybe that's the cruelest part—
not that I can't have you,

but that I know what it feels like
to be yours
in the one way
we're allowed.

I laid my truth
beneath your ribs,
and you kissed it
like a promise
you knew you couldn't keep.

Now I carry you—
not like a regret,
but like a wound
that sings when it rains.
A love
I don't grieve having,
even if I only had it
for a night.

Because you are still
inside me—
in all the ways
you touched
and all the places
you didn't.

Gods Don't Beg

I used to think
being on my knees
meant surrender.
Meant devotion.
Meant love.

But now I know
it meant I'd forgotten
how tall I am.

You knelt too—
but only when it got you
what you craved.
Only when my moans
could answer a prayer
your soul never meant to keep.

And I'm done
begging to be held
like I'm holy.

I am not a confession
you whisper
before sinning again.

I am the god
you never believed in
until you lost me.

Unholy Ghost

You still haunt me,
but not like you used to.

Now you're just a flicker—
a shadow on the wall
when I undress alone,
a whisper I no longer follow.

I used to light candles for you,
pretend the burn was worship.
Now I blow them out
with steady hands.

There's nothing left
to sacrifice.

Redemption

You weren't my punishment.
You were my reflection—
a cracked mirror
I stared into
for too long.

But I see clearly now.

It wasn't love.
It was longing.
It was emptiness wrapped in attention,
praise dipped in possession.

But I forgive myself
for calling it sacred.
Because when we've known so little softness,
even sharp things
can feel like tenderness.

I forgive you too—
not because you earned it,
but because I deserve the freedom
that comes with letting go.

Want, Not Need

I don't need him.

I've already built
a life I love.
I've kissed myself
back to life.
I've danced alone
and laughed like the sky was listening.

But still,
I want him.

Not because he completes me—
but because I'm already whole
and still crave the way
he traces poetry
on my skin.

Wanting,
without losing.

That's the difference now.

Somehow You Found Me

I wasn't supposed
to feel this.
This craving
was meant to be clean—
clinical.
Pleasure
without weight.
Control
without consequence.

But your touch
unstitched something
I swore I buried.

You shouldn't look at me
like that—
like I'm more than the pulse
beneath your fingers.
Like this isn't just a game
I always win.

Because suddenly,
I don't know who's holding who.
And I hate that
I want it to mean something.
That I want *you*
to mean something.

And now I'm the one
with trembling hands
and something to lose.

I Should Have Left Sooner

You lingered.
And I let you.
That was strategy—
not softness.

You looked at me
like you knew me.
Like I was more than
what I let you touch.

And maybe that's why
I kept you longer
than I meant to.
Curiosity,
not care.

I liked the way you looked ruined.
Liked knowing
you'd crawl back to something
I never promised.

But then you got quiet.
And worse—
kind.
And I realized too late:
you weren't playing.

So I ended it.
Not because I had to.
Because I could.

Call it power.
Call it cruelty.
Call it the price
of getting too close

to someone like me.

Don't Stop Praying

You kiss me
like you're making up for lost time.
Like your back forgot
how to be anything but mine.

Your fingers
don't ask permission.
And I don't offer it.
We've never needed
language.

You move
like this is holy ground.
And I swear,
if sin has a sound,
it's your exhale
right before you say my name.

I'm not gentle.
Neither are you.
But somehow,
this still feels sacred.
Like worship
with dirty hands.

So don't stop.

Not now.
Not when you've finally remembered
how to properly pray.

We Don't Come Up for Air

It's not slow
between us.
It never was.

But it's honest—
the way we burn
with the lights off,
like the dark is
permission
to stop pretending
we're anything but starving.

You wrap around me
like a man
who's sure
he won't be forgiven.
And I love you
like a woman
who's done begging
to be holy.

We don't come up for air.
We stay under—
pressed together,
wrecked,
alive.

Only When We're Tangled

You don't talk much
when you're inside me.
But I know what you're saying.

It's in the grip,
the way you bury your face
between my shoulder and regret.
It's in the way
you never leave quietly.

We don't say it out loud.
We don't have to.
The truth only fits
when we're tangled like this—
sweat-slicked,
half-mad,
believing in something
that feels like forever
until we exhale.

You love me best
when words would ruin it.
And I give you everything
I can't say.

I Let You Pray

You reach in my direction
like you're begging forgiveness—
but not from me.
From whatever god
let this happen.

Your pressing
is less about desire
and more about penance.
And I let you pray
in the cathedral
of my thighs,
until your sins forget their names.

There's no salvation here—
just carnage,
just trembling,
just the way your name
leaves my lips
like a final

Amen.

Somewhere Between Holy and Mine

You ask me
what I want
with your mouth
already on me.
As if the answer
isn't obvious.

You ask to worship,
but you like it
when I don't let you.

You pull my hair,
and I call it grace.
I bruise your shoulders,
and you call it proof.
We make a religion
out of ruin,
each kiss
a confessional
no one walks away clean from.

You say my name
like a promise.
I say yours
like a dare.

And in the dark,

between breath and breaking,
we forget
who started praying first.

What You Swore You'd Never Want

You told yourself
you'd never want someone like me.
Too much mouth.
Too much need.
Too much skin
you can't stop tasting
even in your sleep.

But here you are—
on your knees,
voice gone,
praying with your teeth.

You call it obsession.
I call it recognition.
The kind that finds you
when you're too far in
to claw your way out clean.

I am the altar
and the knife.
The ache
and the absolution.
And you—
you're what's left

when men like you
forget who they are
beneath women like me.

Beneath My Mercy

You don't ask
for what you want.
You wait
for me to give it.
And I do—
when I feel like it.

You call it chemistry.
But it's submission,
in a prettier dress.

You beg best
with your body.
Every shiver,
every held scream,
a language you only speak
beneath my mercy.

You say you could leave
anytime.
And I let you believe it.
Because power
tastes better
when the leash
is invisible.

I Name You Mine

You didn't come here to surrender—
but you did.
Slowly.
Beautifully.
Every guarded inch of you
laid down
like an offering.

You wear obedience
like a bruise
you're proud of.
And I trace it
just to remind you
what you are
when you forget.

You try not to need it—
the pressure,
the edge,
the way I see straight through
to the part of you
that never learned
how to want softly.

But it's too late.
You know it.
I've carved myself

into the place
you used to call
control.

And every time you come undone,
you call to me
like a confession.
And I answer
like a god
who always knew
you'd kneel.

When It Feels Like Both

I feel your skin
beneath my teeth—
biting just enough
to blur the line
between pleasure and punishment.

The curve of your shoulder
rests on my lips
like a promise
I'll never get in daylight.

We don't talk about
what this is.
We just move—
gasping for air,
breaking,
trying to outrun
whatever truth waits outside the door.

Because sometimes
fucking feels like love,
and love feels
like fucking—
hot,
hungry,
and holy in all the wrong places.

And I let it.
I let you.
Because in this moment,
we are honest
in the only language
we both know how to speak.

Still Starving

You say you've had enough of me—
but you always come back
with that look in your eyes
like hunger never really leaves.

I give you just enough
to keep you full of desire.
Never enough to be just full.
Never enough to forget.

You wear guilt like cologne
and I take it in.
Call it ritual.
Call it ruin.
Call it ours.

You pretend I'm a mistake.
I pretend I'm not waiting.
We both lie so well
it almost feels like love.

Your Hands Know

You never say the right things.
But your hands—

they remember me.

They move like they've sinned here before.
Trace the edge of my shame
like it's scripture.

You apologize
without a single word,
and I pretend
that's enough.

There's no redemption
in this room.
Just sweat.
And silence.
And bodies that still hesitate
for the wrong reasons.

But I let you in
because part of me still believes
the bruise is proof
that I was ever

touched at all.

The Reckoning

Man Enough

You say you're complicated,
but you're just careless.
You say you're guarded,
but you're just unavailable
and call it depth.

You wear your damage
like armor
and expect me
to praise you
for surviving
what you refuse to unpack.

You think being hard to love
makes you interesting.
But all I see
is a boy
hiding behind excuses
he's polished into personality.

You ask to be worshipped
but not witnessed.
Adored
but never asked to grow.
You want a woman
to raise you
without ever calling it that.

But I'm not your mother.
And you're not a mystery.
You're just a man
who still thinks
emotional illiteracy
is power.

Crown Yourself

You walk like the world owes you something.
Like women should bow
just because you decided to show up.

You crown yourself king
in rooms you didn't build.
Sit on thrones
held up by women
you disrespected.

You demand reverence
while offering nothing
but mood swings,
half-truths,
and hollow silence.

You confuse attention
with effort.
Kindness
with manipulation.
You think control
makes you a man.
But I've met real men—
and they don't cower
when you look them in the eye.

So keep playing powerful
while the rest of us

watch you shrink
every time a woman refuses
to hand you her dignity
like it's a gift.

You can have your pride.
Your stories.
Your throne.

Just know—
you built it out of paper
and crowned yourself
in ashes.

The Tarnished Crown

You spoke of kingdoms, of thrones and might,
Yet your realm was built on borrowed tales,
A sovereign draped in counterfeit robes,
Deceit woven into every thread.

Your words, once honeyed, turned to blades,
Slicing through trust with practiced ease,
Crafting fables where you wore the halo,
While casting me as the shadowed villain.

You stood, a monarch in your own mind,
Demanding fealty unearned,
Forgetting that respect is not bestowed by decree,
But cultivated through honor and truth.

I was not born to be a subject,
Nor to kneel before a fabricated king.
I am the author of my own story,
And you, a footnote in my ascent.

No longer will I dance to your discordant tune,
Nor be ensnared by your tangled lies,
I reclaim the crown you tried to tarnish,
Adorning my spirit with resilience and grace.

What I Almost Said

You asked if I was okay.
And I said yes,
because I always say yes—
even when I'm unraveling quietly
just beneath my throat.

What I almost said was:
I'm tired of pretending I don't feel everything.
Tired of swallowing hurt
so no one else has to taste it.

I almost told you
how hard it is
to hold something real
when real has always come
with an expiration date.

But I just smiled.
And you looked relieved.
And I hated how familiar that felt—
making myself smaller
so someone else could breathe easier.

Storyteller

In the theater of your mind,
you cast yourself the hero,
weaving tales where truth
is but a shadow behind the curtain.
Surrounded by your chorus of nodding heads,
echoes of agreement
drown the dissonance of dissent.

You sculpt reality with forked tongue,
chiseling narratives to fit your mold,
until the lines between fact and fiction blur,
and you stand convinced
of your own fabrications.

But kingdoms built on whispered lies
crumble under the weight of scrutiny.
Respect isn't seized by scepter's decree,
nor worn as an unearned crown.
It's forged in the fires of authenticity,
tempered by deeds, not hollow words.

No throne awaits the self-appointed king
who cloaks insecurity in borrowed robes.
And we, the subjects of your spun stories,
see through the tapestry of deceit,
refusing to bow to a ruler
of a realm that never was.

No One To Blame

I could blame you.
I did—
for a while.
For the way you half-loved me,
for the silences,
the exits,
the cowardice dressed as conflict.

But now I see it.
You never lied to me.
You just weren't capable
of more than pieces.

And I'm done
trying to make a whole man
out of fragments.

You were never mine.
You were never ready.
And I?
I was always too much
for someone
who craved to feel big
without ever being brave.

Lonely Beside You

There's nothing lonelier
than lying next to someone
who doesn't see you anymore.
Than whispering *I'm fine*
into a silence
that stopped listening a long time ago.

You reached for me
like you were checking a box,
like routine had replaced wonder,
and I was just
what waited on the other side
of a long day.

I used to count your movements
like prayers.
Now I count the spaces
where your warmth
used to be.
I stayed—
long after I should have,
because even emptiness
feels familiar
when it's wearing someone
you loved.

I Saw The Red Flags

I saw them.
Every single one.
But I made them blush
into something softer,
something I could live with.

You said things
that scraped against my gut,
and I called it passion.
You pulled away,
and I called it space.
You hurt me,
and I called it love
with jagged edges.

I wanted so badly
to make you the right one
that I abandoned the parts of me
that knew better.
But I know now:
ignoring my own truth
was the deepest wound of all—
and I will never again
bleed for someone
who won't even bruise.

The Distance in Your Eyes

You were inches away,
and still,
I couldn't reach you.
I tried—
with my laughter,
with the curve of my hips,
with all the softness I had left.

But you looked at me
like I was furniture—
familiar,
useful,
silent.

I used to crave your gaze.
Now I flinch from it.
Not because it's cold,
but because it doesn't search
for anything in me anymore.

We shared a bed,
meals,
plans.
But not presence.
Not the kind that matters.

And somehow,

that was lonelier
than any night I've spent
alone.

To The One After Me

You won't see it at first.
He's good at the beginning.
Charming.
Thoughtful.
Like someone who listens.

But pay attention
to how often he rewrites
what you say.
How silence
becomes your new language.
How your name
starts to feel
like a compromise.

He will call himself loyal
while still carrying
the tools to dismantle you.

He'll blame his past
for the mess he makes of you.

He'll say he loves women—
but only if they're soft,
forgiving,
and smaller than him
in every room.

You'll think you're the exception.
We all did.

Just don't lose yourself
trying to prove it.

You Call It Respect

You call it respect—
but only when it's handed to you.
Only when a woman is quiet,
agreeable,
small.

You call it disrespect
when she asks for more.
When she speaks up.
When she sees through you.

You think being a man
means being obeyed.

But a real man
doesn't confuse
intimidation
with strength.

We're not hard to love.
You're just too fragile
to be met on equal ground.

I Wasn't Miscommunication

It wasn't miscommunication.
You heard me just fine—
you just didn't like the sound
of a woman who wouldn't shrink.

You wanted someone
who'd stay quiet,
smile pretty,
and call it love.

I asked for honesty.
You offered excuses.
I asked for depth.
You got defensive.

So I left.
Not because I was confused—
but because I finally saw
how small you are
when you're not in control.

I Don't Hate You, You're Just Small

You think I hate you.
I don't.
You're just small.
Smaller than your words.
Smaller than your promises.
Smaller than the mask
you kept adjusting
every time I got too close.

I didn't leave because you were broken.
I left because you were comfortable staying that way.

You call me cold.
But I only stopped handing warmth
to someone who mistook it
for weakness.

You don't have enemies.
You have mirrors—
and you smash

every single one
that doesn't flatter you.

So no,
I don't hate you.
But I do see you now.
And that's worse.

You Didn't Do Anything Wrong

You walk into rooms
like volume is virtue.
Like being the loudest
makes you right.
Like being a man
makes you the center.

But your voice
was always bigger than your character.
Your opinions
always sharper than your self-awareness.

You confuse intimidation
with leadership,
and silence
with submission.
You thought my patience
was praise.

You want to be respected
just for showing up.
For existing.
For wearing the title
without ever doing the work.

And when I finally left—
when I was done
translating your tantrums

into truth—
you looked me dead in the eye
and said:
"I didn't do anything wrong."

And you were right.
You didn't do anything at all.
Not a single thing
that looked like love.
Not one act
that resembled growth.
You did nothing—
and still expected everything.

So wear that sentence
like a badge.
Make it your anthem.

It's the truest thing
you've ever said.

You'll Be Back

You always come back
after the damage is done.
Once the silence
starts to echo.
Once you realize
no one else
will swallow the version of you
you wish was true.

You come back
with tired eyes,
half-apologies,
and that same line:
"I've been thinking."

I bet you have.
I bet it's loud in there
without my voice
telling you you're good
when you're not.

But I don't miss you anymore.
Not even a little.
Not even when it's quiet.
Not even when I'm lonely.

You'll be back.
And I'll be better.

Not bitter.
Not broken.
Just…
already gone.

King of Nothing

You don't want love.
You want worship.
A woman to kneel
not because she adores you—
but because you believe she should.

You want power
without responsibility.
Respect,
without earning it.

You say you're a king,
but you rule from a paper throne,
built on victimhood
and empty declarations.

You demand loyalty
while offering none,
raise your voice
when met with truth,
and run
when faced with consequence.

You want to be honored
just for existing.
But crowns are heavy,
and yours was stolen.

You're no king—
just a boy in borrowed armor,
hiding behind stories
that only serve
to keep you small.

False Prophet

You wear goodness
like a costume—
stitched it to your skin
so no one sees
what's crawling underneath.

Always the nice guy.
Always the one who's misunderstood.
You turn every scar
into a stage,
every conflict
into a monologue
where you're always
the one bleeding.

But I saw it—
the cracks in your kindness,
the way your charm
only lasted
as long as I kept quiet.

You don't want a partner.
You want a twisted mirror.
Something to reflect
the version of you
you tell the world is real.

You pretended to be gentle—
but it was just another way
to silence me.

And when I stopped shrinking,
you called it cruelty.
Painted yourself innocent,
while your hands stayed clean
and your words did the damage.

But you don't get to weaponize
your weakness
and call it virtue.

Gone

You craved control,
not closeness.
Obedience,
not connection.

You didn't want to love me—
you wanted to win.

And now that I'm gone,
you want access
to the version of me
you never earned.
The one who bent.
Softened.
Waited.

But she's gone.
Buried beneath every time
you made her feel too much
for asking
for the bare minimum.

So no—
you don't get to come back.
You don't get to miss me
from afar
and call it growth.

You get to wonder
how I taste in someone else's mouth.
How my laugh sounds
with someone who listens.
How it feels
to be replaced
by someone who doesn't fall apart
when faced with a whole woman.

You wanted power.
Now all you have
is silence.

Burn The Letter

I hope you burn the letter I wrote.
It hurts to know I was that blind—
that I didn't see through the veil of lies.

I let you lead me
to a safety
that was never safe,
because you don't know
what safe spaces are made of.
Everything you create
is chaos on blank pages,
crafted to convince us
the lines are straight.

But you're twisted—
spilling over in victimhood,
living in broken corners
of a half-finished house
and a mind that skips.

You keep petty in your back pocket,
pull it out to shape
a louder narrative.

You lied the loudest,
convincing the world you were quiet.

Puffed the biggest,
pretending we believed you were secure.

You fall the hardest—
because the good ones
will always figure it out.

You can't hide forever
the *Nothing*
that you are.

Burn The Books

I hope you burn my books.
You should no longer have access
to any part of me—
past or present.

My words
should be banned from your eyes,
erased from your lips.

Every sentence you once praised
should turn to ash
before it ever reaches your tongue.

My pages
deserve better floors
than yours to fall on.
Better hands
than yours to hold them.

May the fire singe your fingertips
every time you try to remember
how I felt.

You don't get to carry my stories
in your pocket
like a souvenir of something
you never honored.

You lost the right
to know my voice.
To speak it.
To touch it.

You don't get to long for the parts of me
you helped break.

So burn it all.
And when the flames rise,
remember:
you don't get to keep
what you never truly saw.

Almost Yours

Haunted Spaces

I break in the spaces
you refuse to fill,
make love to the ghosts
of what we almost were,
and wonder
if you ever close your eyes
and see me there—
ruinous,
waiting,
yours.

In the quiet of midnight's hush,
your absence presses against me,
a phantom limb I cannot unfeel.
I reach into the void,
fingers grazing memories
that dissolve like mist,
leaving only the scent
of what could have been.

Your silence carves hollows
into the marrow of my days,
each moment stretched taut
with the weight of unsaid words.
Yet, in this emptiness,

I find a perverse solace,
a sanctuary built
from the echoes of you.

The Last Time I Let You In

You came to me
like you always do—
with that look,
with that voice,
with those hands
that know too much of me.

But this time,
something inside me stayed cold.
Still.
Watching.

Your kiss didn't taste like magic.
It tasted like history—
repeating itself.
Movement on autopilot.
A habit pretending to be a heartbeat.

And I let it happen,
but not like before.
Not hoping.
Not waiting.
Just…
finishing.

You didn't notice.
But I did.
This was the last time

you'd be allowed
to confuse my need
for love.

You'll Miss Me Later

Not now.
Not when she's next to you,
asking what you want for dinner.

But one day,
when the silence feels too loud
and her touch feels too clean,
you'll think of me.

Of the mess.
The madness.
The way I never asked you
to be anything
but real.

You'll remember my breath
against your throat,
the sound I made
when I broke for you,
again and again—
and how I still kissed you
like I believed you were better
than all of this.

And maybe then,
you'll realize
you were deeply loved

by the one person
who never needed you

to cover up.

Clarity

It didn't come with screaming.
It came with stillness.
The kind that follows
after a storm
when the debris
tells the truth.

I saw it all—
every half-promise,
every time you looked away
instead of stepping closer.

And somehow,
I loved you more in that moment
than I ever had.
Because I finally saw you.

Small.
Scared.
Unwilling.

And I?
I am not a woman
you visit in the dark
to remember who you almost were.

I am the light
you were never brave enough
to live in.

What I Know Now

I know now
that being chosen
isn't a prize
if it comes at the cost
of my peace.

I know the difference
between desire and devotion,
between flesh and soul,
between begging and being held.

You taught me that—
not with love,
but with absence.
Not with truth,
but with your fear of it.

And for that,
strangely,
I thank you.
Because now I choose me—
the full, feral,
fire-breathing version
you were never strong enough
to stand beside.

Rewritten

I took the story
you gave me—
the one where I was the secret,
the soft place,
the shame.

And I rewrote it.

Now,
I am the woman
who walked away
before the ruin.
The one who turned hunger
into wholeness,
who turned your silence
into her own song.

You don't get to haunt me.
You don't get to linger.
Your chapter is closed,
filed under fiction.

And me—
I'm writing poetry again.
But not for you.

Never again for you.

Hard To Hold

I want to be held,
but I don't know how to loosen
without bracing
for the break.

Even kindness
makes me flinch sometimes—
not because I don't crave it,
but because I don't trust
it'll stay.

People have left
after tasting the quiet in me,
after brushing up against
the parts I don't show right away.

And so I've learned
to curl inward,
to smile when I'm scared,
to make myself easy
to walk away from.

But still,
some small part of me hopes
someone will stay—
not just when I'm bright,
but when I'm bruised.

Someone who won't
make me shrink
to be loved.

Not Easy

I'm not easy to love.
Not because I don't want it,
but because I've known
what it feels like
to be loved conditionally—
to be cherished
until I needed too much
or said the wrong thing
or bled in front of someone
who only craved the light.

So now,
I test the water
with one toe,
even when my heart
is already drowning.
I laugh
when I mean stay.
I close up
right when I want to be held.

And I hate it.
But it's the only way
I know how to survive
without unraveling.

Closer Than I Meant

I let you in
further than I meant to.
It was subtle—
a word,
a glance,
the way your hand rested
on the back of my neck
like you were trying to calm
a storm you didn't even know
was there.

And for a moment,
I believed you might stay.
Not because you said it,
but because your quiet
didn't feel like absence.

But hope is a tricky thing.
It makes promises
no one ever speaks aloud.
It carves space
for something that may never come.

Still—
you reached me.
Even if just for a moment.

And that moment
still lives
in the softest part of me.

I Still Want To Believe

Some days,
I don't trust the good.
Kindness feels like a trick,
like something I'll have to pay for later.

But I still want to believe—
in warmth without condition,
in love that doesn't come
with a list of requirements,
in someone who chooses me
without needing me
to shrink.

I want laughter in a kitchen
with no eggshells underfoot.
I want silence
that doesn't feel like punishment.

And most of all,
I want to stop questioning
whether I deserve
what I keep reaching for.

I Betrayed Myself First

Before you broke me,
I'd already started
chipping away at who I was—
sanding down my edges
so I could fit inside
what you wanted.

I laughed when I was hurting.
Stayed when I was starving.
Bit my tongue
until it forgot how to speak.

I told myself
this was love—
the sacrifice,
the shrinking,
the emptiness.

But the truth is,
you didn't have to destroy me.
I handed you the hammer.

The Lie I Told Myself

I told myself
you were trying.
That your silence
was thoughtful,
that your distance
was temporary,
that your cruelty
was just pain
you hadn't learned
how to hold.

But the truth is,
you weren't trying.
Not really.

You were comfortable.
And I was convenient.
And I stayed—
because I thought
loving you
meant proving I was worthy
of being chosen.

But I see now—
the only person
who ever needed to choose me
was me.

Still Here

I came back to myself
like a survivor—
mud on my knees,
truth in my mouth.

Not whole,
but real.
Not healed,
but healing.

I stopped asking
why it happened.
Stopped trying to fix
what was never mine to carry.

Now,
I run my hands
over the parts of me
I used to hide,
and say,
You're still here.
And that is enough.

Nothing to Prove

I don't need to be wanted
to feel worthy.
Don't need to be chosen
to believe I matter.

I don't chase anymore.
I don't audition.
I don't ask for love
in places it can't exist.

I let go of needing
to be enough
for someone else
just to believe
I'm enough for me.

There is power
in not performing.

And peace
in no longer proving
what's already true.

I Am The Constant

They left.
They changed.
They lied.
They failed to see me.
And still—
I remained.

Bent, maybe.
Bruised, definitely.
But never broken.
Never gone.

Through every goodbye,
every apology that never came,
every night I held myself
because no one else did—
I stayed.

And now I know:
I am the constant.
The home.
The light.
The thing I was always looking for.

Something Like Beginning

It's not that I'm unafraid—
I've just decided
fear doesn't get to be the one
holding the pen.

So I let you in,
inch by inch,
watching your eyes
for the flicker of departure
that used to come so fast.

But it doesn't.
You stay.
And I breathe.

Not deeply,
not yet.
But enough.

Enough to believe
this might be
something different.
Something slow.
Something real.

The Risk

Loving again
feels like walking into a storm
without an umbrella—
knowing what it could cost,
but craving the rain anyway.

I don't need you
to save me.
I've done that already.

But if you're willing
to meet me here—
in the place where my guard lowers
one heartbeat at a time—
then stay.

I'll be scared.
I'll overthink.
I'll have days
where I forget I'm safe.

But I'll try.
I'll show up.
And I'll love you
like a woman
who finally knows her worth.

Because I do.

If I Let You In

If I let you in,
know this:
I'm not asking you
to fix what broke.

I've stitched myself up
in too many dark rooms
to believe healing comes
from someone else's hands.

But I am asking
for gentleness.
For patience.
For the kind of quiet
that doesn't feel
like punishment.

I don't want perfect.
I just want honest.
Present.
Steady.

If you can be that—
you can come closer.

Just... don't knock
unless you mean to stay.

You Didn't Run

I told you the truth—
the messy version,
the one with jagged edges
and stories I don't tell
to just anyone.

And you didn't run.
Didn't flinch.
Didn't try to make it pretty.

You just listened,
like the weight of me
wasn't something
you feared carrying.

And I didn't say thank you—
not out loud.
But I softened,
just a little,
in the places I thought
had hardened for good.

This Is What It Feels Like

To be touched
without being used.
To be heard
without being handled.
To be wanted
with no strings
pulling me into someone else's version
of who I should be.

This is what it feels like—
to laugh
without watching for the exit,
to feel safe
in the silence,
to trust someone
and not lose myself.

And I didn't know
love could be this quiet
and still be true.

But here you are.
And here I am.
Still me.
Finally seen.

Slow Is Sacred

I used to think
love had to be fast—
a flood,
a fire,
a storm that swept me
into forgetting.

But this time,
it's different.
You come to me
like water rising—
slow, steady,
certain.

And I don't lose myself
in the tide.
I find pieces
I didn't know I'd left behind.

There is no urgency
in your eyes.
Only invitation.
Only patience.

And I am learning
that slow love
can be the deepest kind—

the kind that lasts
because it never asks me
to disappear.

Taking Back

I took back my voice.
The one I buried
to make others comfortable.
The one I quieted
so love wouldn't leave.

I took back my body.
No longer a bargaining chip,
no longer a place
for someone else's shame
to take shelter.

I took back my soul.
Unashamed.
Unapologetic.
Unfolding.

This is what it means
to return to yourself—
not unscarred,
but unashamed.

I do not belong
to anyone
who cannot hold me
without asking me
to disappear.

In Another Life, This Is Ours

With you,
I don't have to explain.
You read between my silences
like they're written for you.
And maybe they are.

You see the parts of me
I usually hide—
the too-much,
the not-enough,
the soft that's always bracing for impact.
And you don't flinch.
You lean in.

There's something about you
that quiets the noise.
That makes even the broken places
feel holy.

You ask nothing from me
except truth.
And I give it to you—
easily,
completely,
like I've been waiting
my whole life
to be this known.

We talk like dreamers.
Whisper a life
we'll never get to live.
What we'd cook.
Where we'd go.
How we'd love
without fear
or walls
or time limits.

Sometimes I see it so clearly
it feels like a memory.
A home I've never stepped inside
but somehow miss
every day.

I know we can't have it.
Not here.
Not now.

But somewhere—
in some softer timeline—
this isn't longing.
It's real.
It's ours.
And we never had to ask
if it was allowed.

What We Could Be

When we're together,
it's like the world falls away.
Like we're the only two
who ever learned how to speak
without needing words.

I don't have to hide.
Not the parts of me that tremble,
not the ones that burn.
You've seen them all—
the bits of me I don't share
with anyone else.
And you still choose me.
Still see me.
Still love me.

In your eyes,
I am enough.
And when I close mine,
I can almost feel
the life we could have had.
The mornings,
the quiet hours,
the moments that have no labels,
no explanations.
Just us—

taking up space
in ways no one else ever could.

I want that life with you.
I want the time we've never had—
the freedom to grow,
to stretch into the spaces
that no one else fills.

I want to give you all of me,
to live alongside you
in a world we make together,
where nothing is held back
and everything is shared.

But for now,
we are just
what we are—
a deep connection,
a need only we can meet,
and the quiet dream
of what could have been.

Almost

I saw you today.
And everything in me
stood still.

Not just my breath—
my bones.
My memory.
My resolve.

You looked at me
like the world fell away,
but your life didn't.

And I smiled.
Because I love you.
Still.
Even here.
Even now.
Even with all this distance
and the quiet between us.

We said nothing—
but our eyes
remembered everything.

There was love.
There is love.

But not a single step
between us.

Because some things
are too sacred
to ruin
with reality.

I Am The Ending

There is no great crescendo,
no applause,
no tidy ribbon to tie it all.

Just me.
Still standing.
Still soft.
Still sacred.

The story didn't end
when he left,
or when I stayed,
or when I broke.

It ends here—
with me
choosing myself
without needing
anyone else to agree.

I am not the aftermath.
I am the main character.
I am the plot twist.

I am the ending
I was always looking for.

About The Author

Jessica Kristie is a poet and author drawn to the spaces where love bruises and longing lingers. Her work explores themes of passion, abandonment, emotional healing, and reclamation.

You can find her on her website or social media, where her voice continues to reach many through words that cut deep, and soothe, all at once.

JessicaKristie.com
TikTok: JessKristie
IG: JessicaKristie

www.ingramcontent.com/pod-product-compliance
Lightning Source LLC
Chambersburg PA
CBHW030826090426
42737CB00009B/897